The Longest Winter

MW01686946

The Longest Winter
Photographs and artist statement copyright © 1999 Julie Doiron
Fiction text and artist statement copyright © 1999 Ian Roy
Afterword copyright © 1999 Joe Blades

Acknowledgements: Several of these photos have been or will be published in *Exclaim!*, *CHSR Soundcheck* and with Julie Doiron's CD *Will You Still Love Me?* (Tree Records). A photo and text selection from the book was published in *New Muse of Contempt* magazine.

No part of this publication may be reproduced, stored in a retrieval system or transmitted, in any form or by any means, without the prior written permission of the publisher or, in the case of photocopying or other reprographic copying, a licence from the Canadian Copyright Licencing Agency (CAN©OPY), 1900-1 Yonge St, Toronto ON M5E 1E5. Tel (416) 868-1620, 1-800-893-5777, admin@cancopy.com www.cancopy.com

In-house editing by the publisher, Joe Blades
Layout by Joe Blades based upon design concept by Jon Claytor
Most of the photographs were scanned at Prolab, Fredericton. Thanks, Rob
Printed and bound in Canada by Centennial Print, Fredericton NB

The publisher gratefully acknowledges the support of the Canada Council for the Arts and the Arts Development Branch-New Brunswick Department of Economic Development, Tourism and Culture.

THE CANADA COUNCIL FOR THE ARTS SINCE 1957 | LE CONSEIL DES ARTS DU CANADA DEPUIS 1957

Canadian Cataloguing in Publication Data
Doiron, Julie 1972-

The longest winter

ISBN: 0-921411-95-2

1. Artist's books — Canada. 2. Photography, Artistic. I. Roy, Ian, 1972-
II. Title.

TR6890.D63 1999 779'.092 C99-950175-5

Broken Jaw Press
Box 596 Stn A
Fredericton NB E3B 5A6
Canada
www.brokenjaw.com
jblades@nbnet.nb.ca
tel / fax 506 454-5127

The Longest Winter

photographs by Julie Doiron
words by Ian Roy

Broken Jaw Press
Fredericton • Canada

Acknowledgements

We would like to thank everyone who appears in this book and anyone who has ever let Julie photograph them. Also we want to thank Peter Rowan for introducing us to Joe Blades, Joe for wanting to do this, and Jon Claytor for all his help and suggestions with the book as well as in life. And, finally, thank you to Sarah Caspi, Max, Ben and Charlotte.

for
Charlotte, Ben and Max

Artist Statements

My words could never match my photos and so I thank Ian for wanting to add his to them. Through these photographs I've said what I can and I hope they say as much to you as they do to me.

A self-portrait.

Cold and lonely. Though not without love. Despair yet such hope. And my children. So naturally bright and beautiful and wanting to be here with us. Making it so much easier to be here.

Take care of yourselves. All of you. It will eventually pass.

— Julie Doiron

Julie contacted me about doing this project some time ago. I was already familiar with many of the photographs. There is a quality to them that suggests to me another time and place; but a feeling, too, of looking forward, expectantly, hopefully — sometimes sadly.

Looking at the photographs, I was overwhelmed by feelings of nostalgia, even though these photographs are of my contemporaries and their children. I thought of how things just never work out the way you plan. I also imagined our own children looking back at these photographs and piecing together their own lives — and ours — from the fragments and stills: an attempt to understand the life that was, that is. I realized, too, as I looked at these photographs that many of the memories from my childhood have turned out to be photographs, snapshots taken by someone else.

It is not a condemnation, nor is it like the sad repetition of a skipping record. It is both a remembering and a forgetting, a reminiscence and a nod to the future: an acknowledgment of the circularity of this life; and a recognition that history repeats itself again and again. Nothing changes, I kept thinking, everything stays the same. But while this is true, we are different people with our own problems and concerns and, of course, loves. We are trying again.

The collaboration became a point of maintaining and expressing that mood that was created for me by these intimate — almost private — photographs. The writing is meant to accompany the photographs in an elliptical interchange: together, they tell a story.

— Ian Roy

Prologue

Sometimes there is nothing more sad, more despairing than wanting to recover the past. When memories add up like numbers, when they are so strong they have a smell, a taste or a texture, when they can bring you to your knees, it is difficult to turn away from them and continue walking into an uncertain future — because really, it is all very uncertain and scary and sometimes, if you are unlucky, it is also lonely.

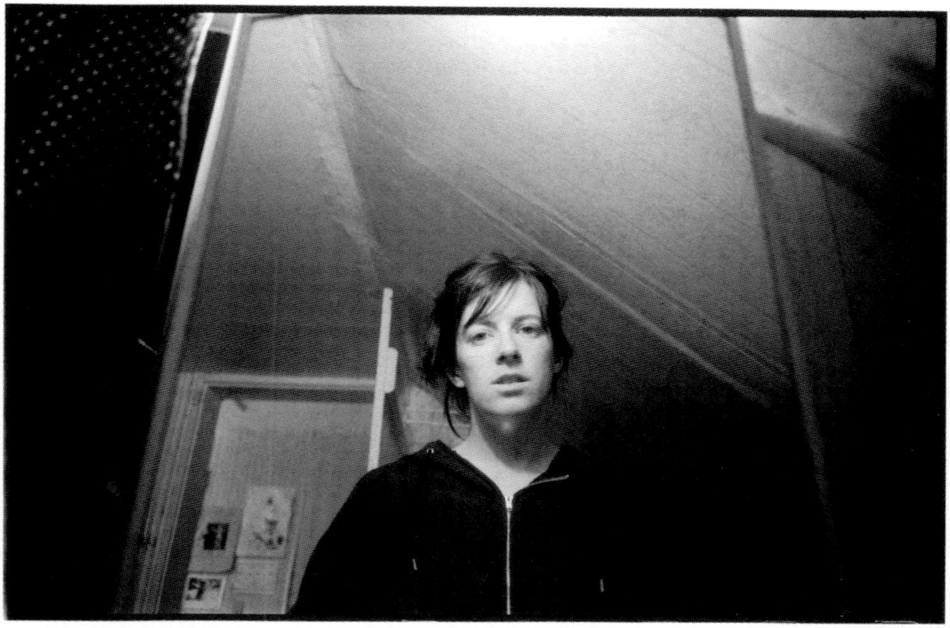

The theatre was dark when I arrived. I found an empty seat by the aisle and sat down. The movie was French, subtitled. It was about people leaving: sons leaving mothers, lovers leaving lovers. Some words and phrases were not translated, ignored. A man holding a photograph of a beautiful, young woman was being chased around a table by an old woman carrying a butcher's knife. It was meant to be funny. *Mais maman, ce n'est pas juste. J'aime Monique. Maman, c'est l'amour!* As I watched the screen, the characters began to blur in their circular movement — round and round the table in frenzied circles. I began to feel dizzy. I closed my eyes and for some reason, I thought of you.

Sometimes I feel closest to you — with these years and miles and life and even, this is sad, death between us — looking at photographs you took, and photographs of you. Years separate that time from this time, that person from the person you are, all of us are.

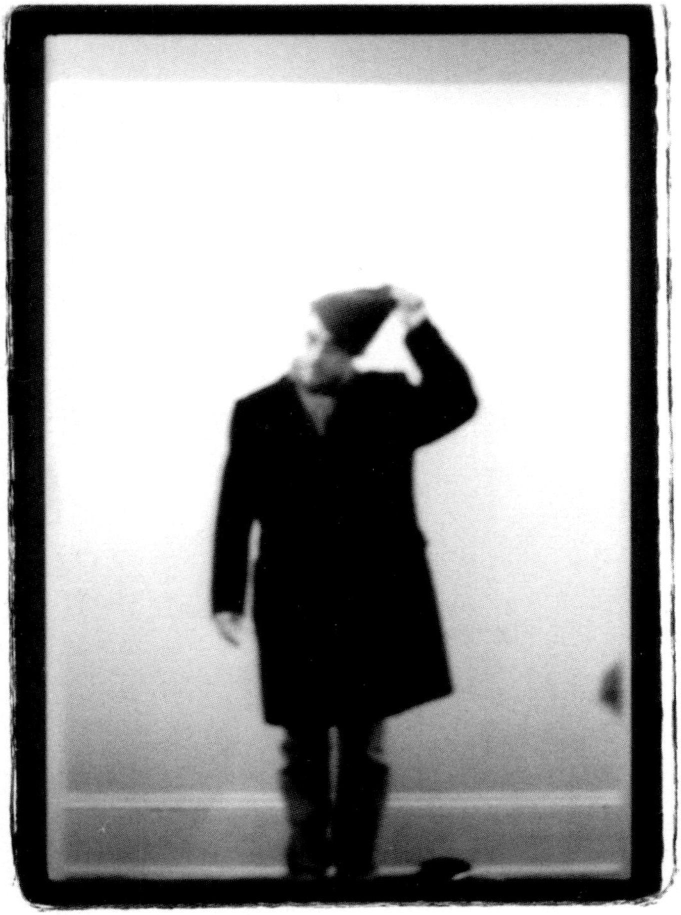

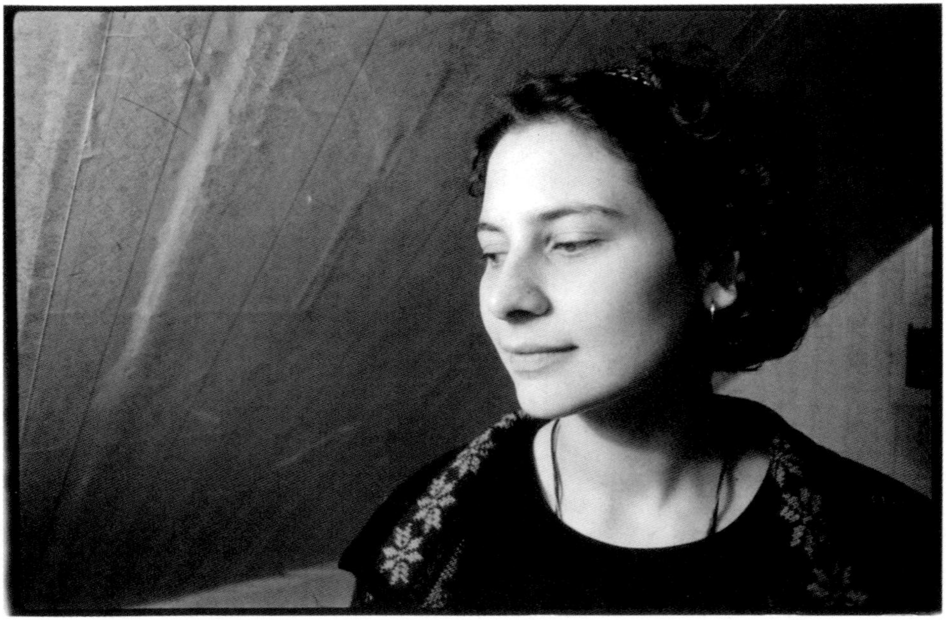

But I must remember, when looking at a photograph, that it is only a slip of paper I hold in my hand. And if it were left out in the rain, well, you know what would happen, don't you? After a long time, a photograph fades the same way a memory does.

We'd sit for hours, you and I, talking about nothing much at all. Slowly, your hand would fall on my knee and you'd laugh. And then I'd laugh. My hand would fall on your hand. And we'd just sit there, talking about nothing much at all. The sun would have set hours before. Or maybe it would be closer to sunrise but we'd keep sitting there, waiting for something to happen. And eventually it did. Look at us now.

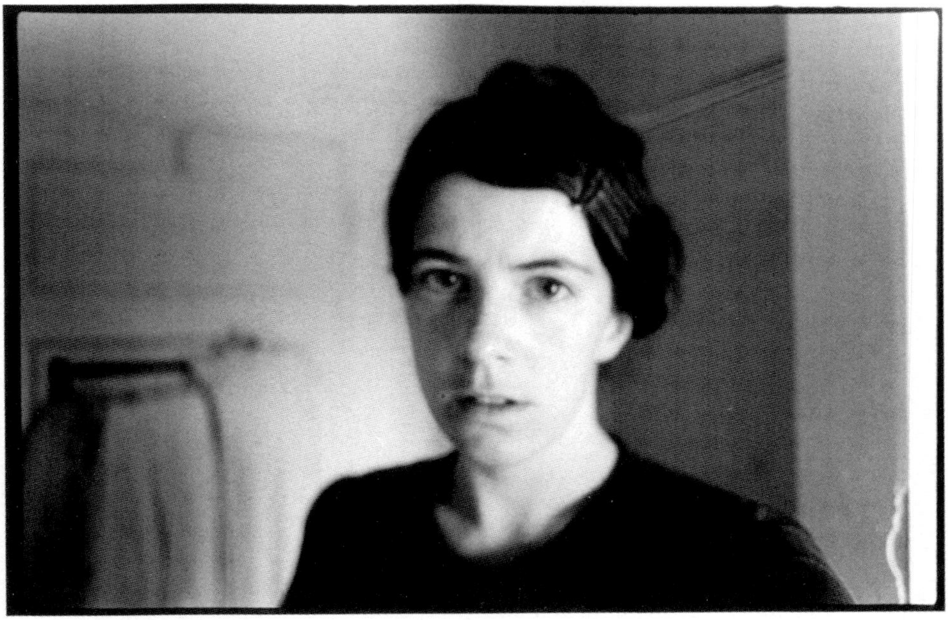

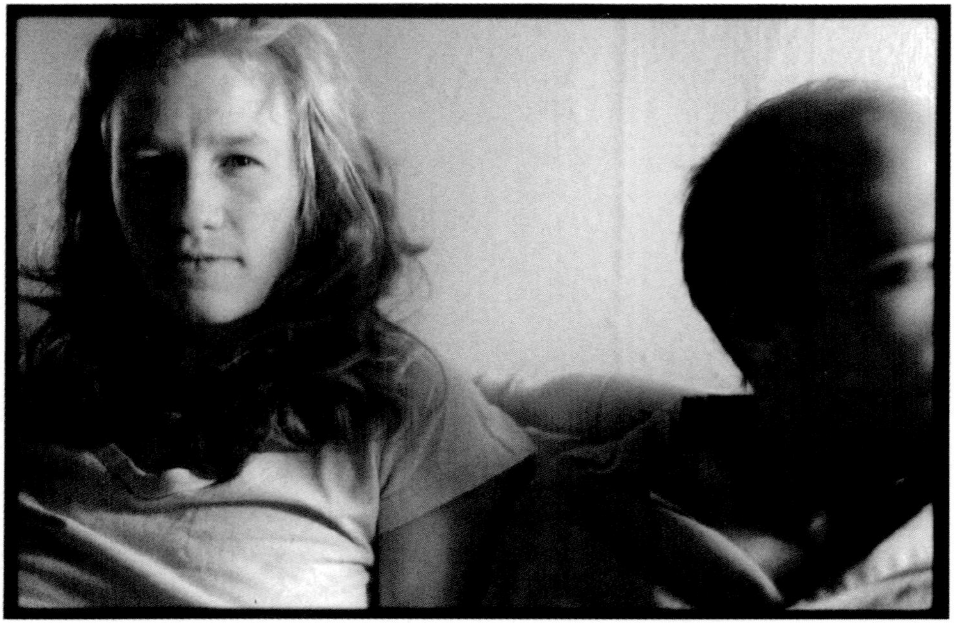

A house of cards, you said. *That is closer to a memory, a memory is closer to that. You just blow and...*

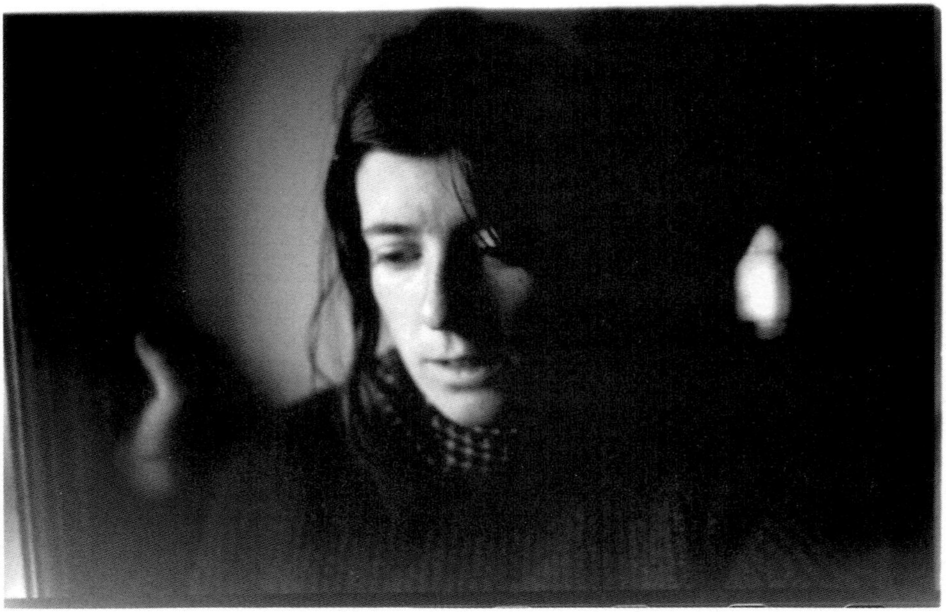

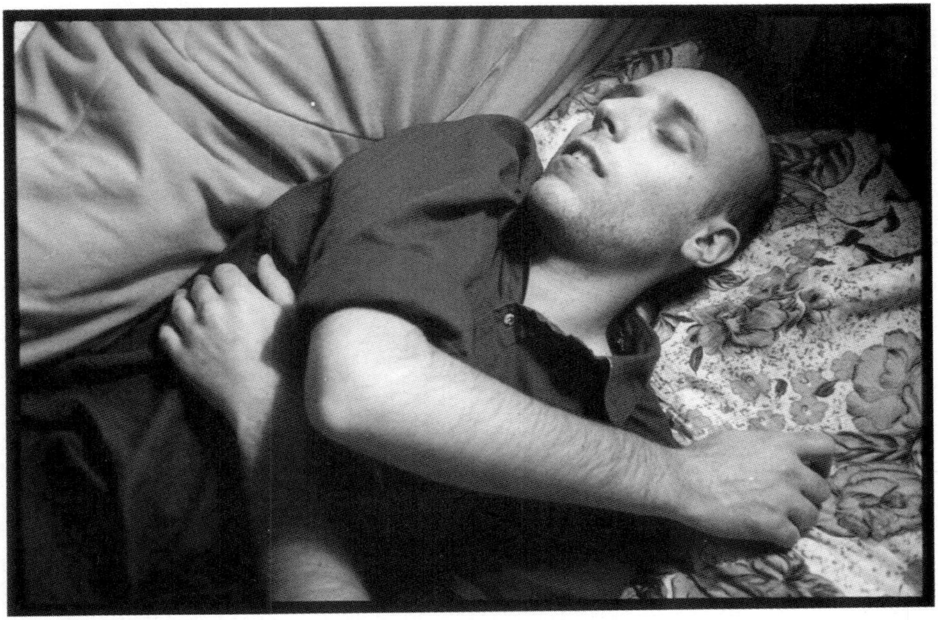

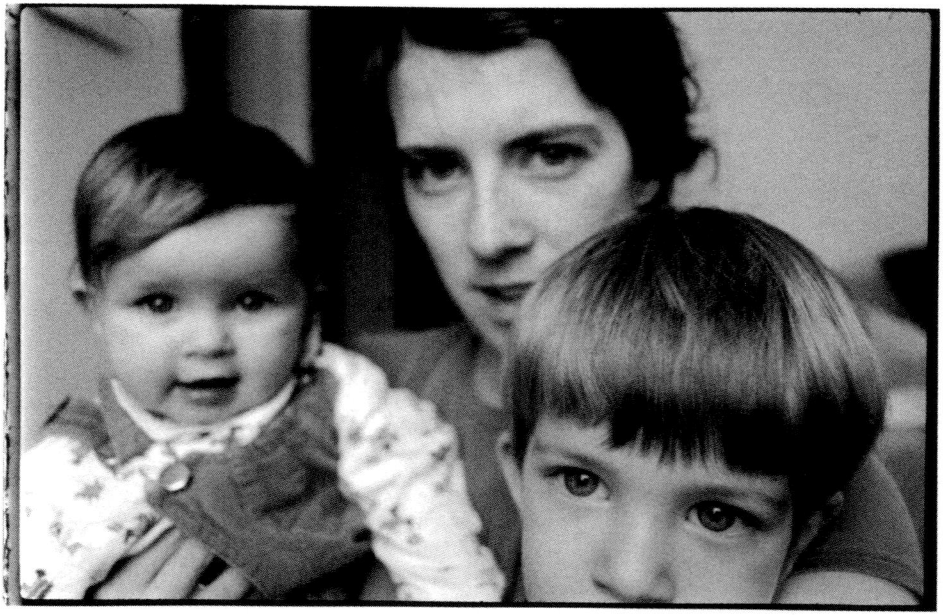

They weren't all mistakes. No. Some shine, eclipsing everything and everyone, with a brilliance that can only be found in the simplest (the most complex?) gesture.

They help us to forget, and to remember; to be in two places at once: I am here with you now; I am there where I was. But that is not what you want to hear, not even what I want to say. And as I write it, I wonder at its truthfulness, its sincerity. I remember pieces of advice given to me at different times, and how they never seemed to help. If they had been rocks, I would have thrown them at a window, any window.

Once, when I was younger, I tried to put a hole in a wall using only my bare hand. I know, I know: it is funny. I didn't even make a dent. But listen...

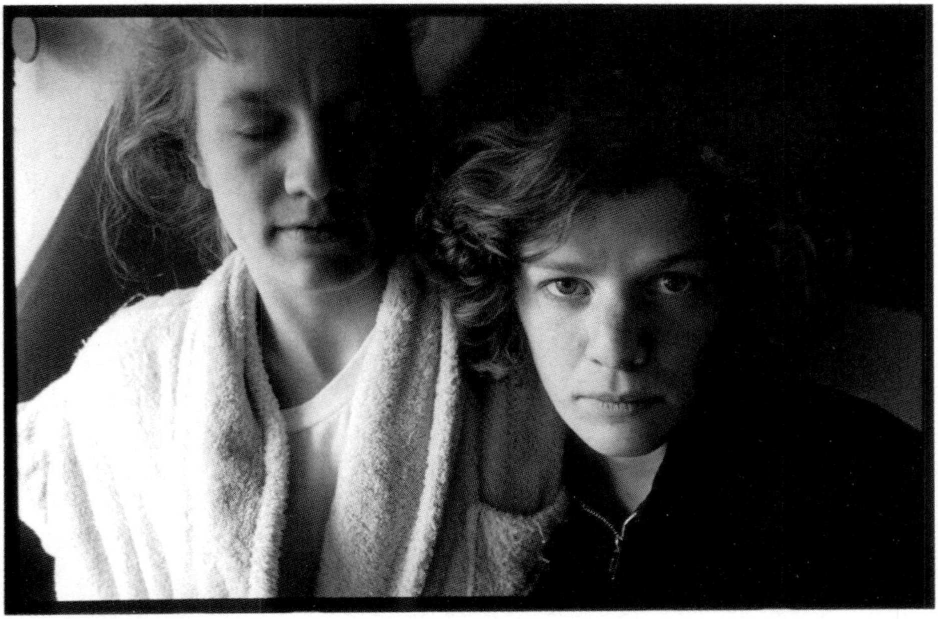

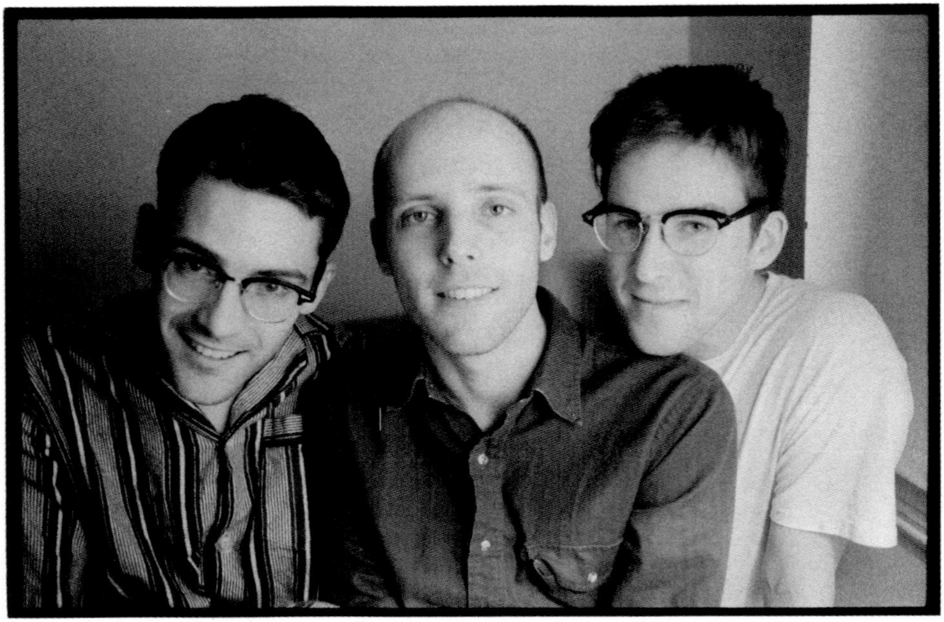

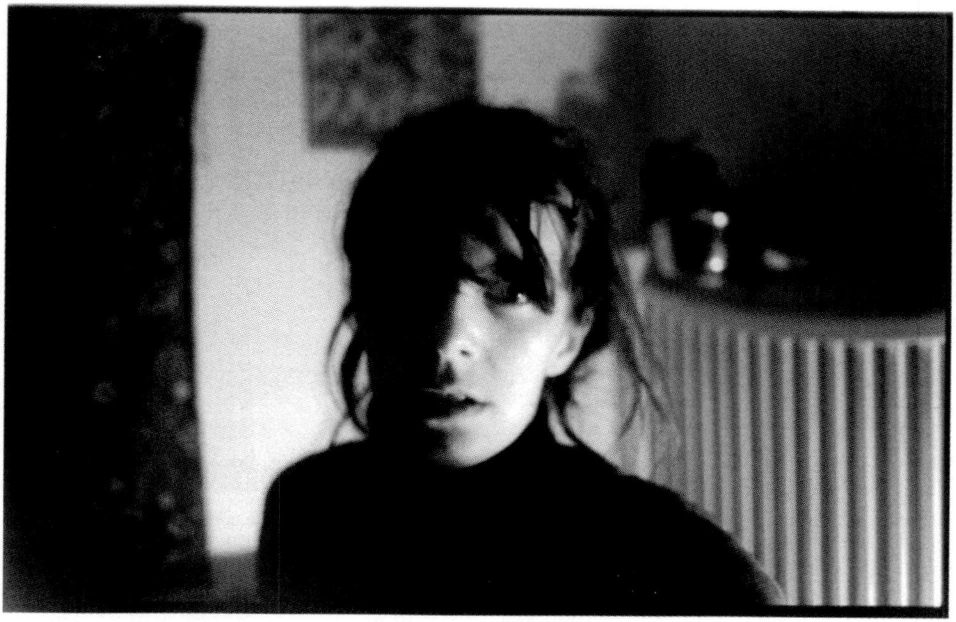

Every year I make the same discoveries, only to spend the whole of the next year forgetting. And then discovering for a too-brief time what I once knew, only to forget again. It goes on like that, my past, our past: the same mistakes when I forget, and the same ones when I remember. Someone once pointed out to me that you must forget in order to remember. Was that you? Someone.

There is little we can do to dredge up that past, and really, who would want to? Me? It would appear so because here I am thinking of you: searching for a piece, a hint, a glimmer. The slightest evidence would send me home, not necessarily smiling — but home. Wherever that is now.

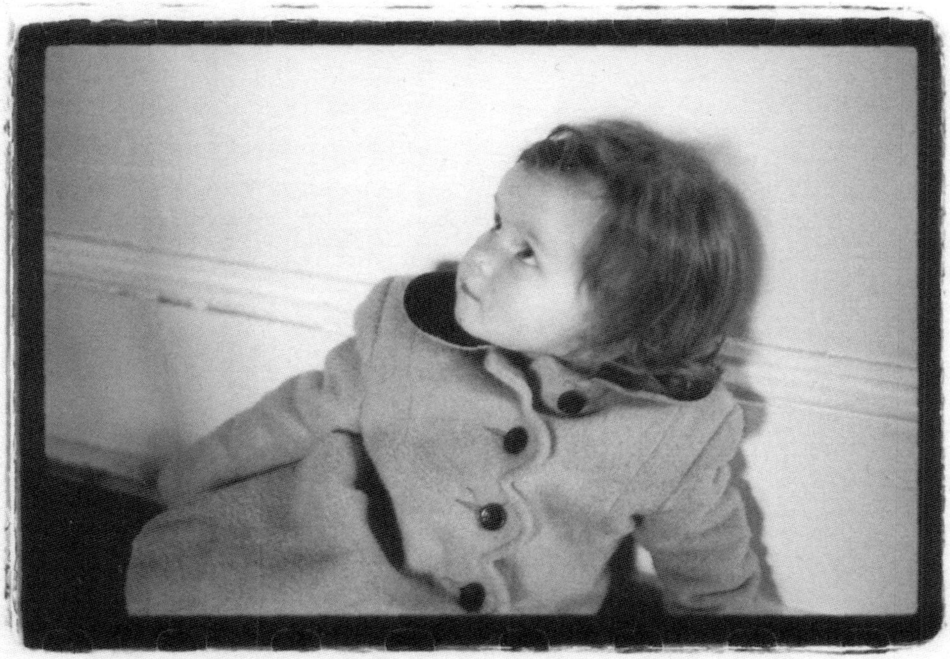

Before you left that time, I wanted to be out of the house and far away. I guess I didn't want to have to say goodbye: I get so sad when people leave, and it would be no different with you. But I stayed and helped you with your coat. The tag read *L'il Nugget* and you said, *that's just what I am*. And then you walked on ahead and down the stairs and outside into the sunlight. I watched from the window: something I would get used to.

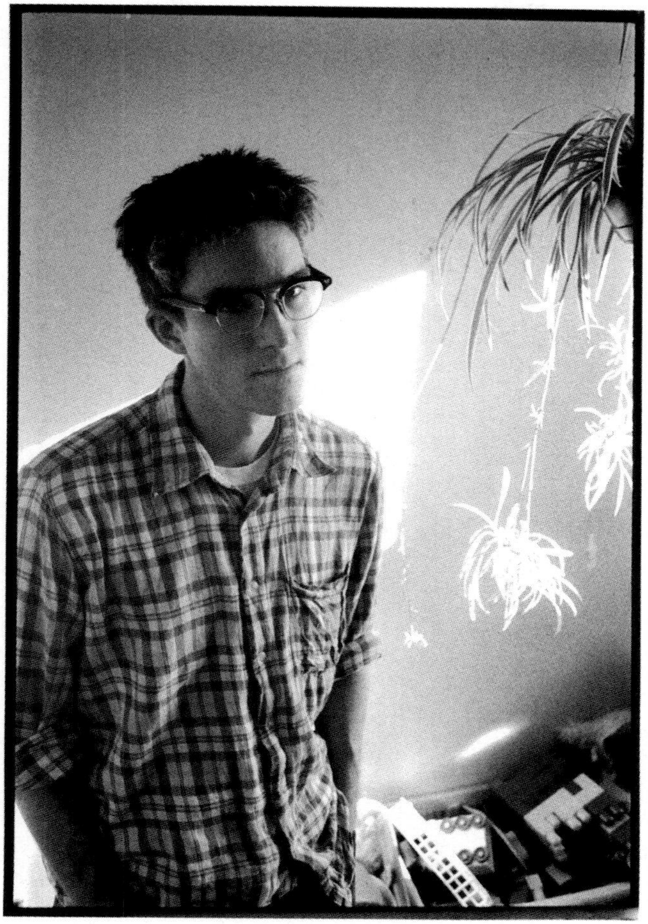

(The radio was always on there and at times it was all you could hear — not the vacuum, not the snowplough scraping against the asphalt outside, not crying — just the radio playing. Voices singing songs. Singing voices, songs.)

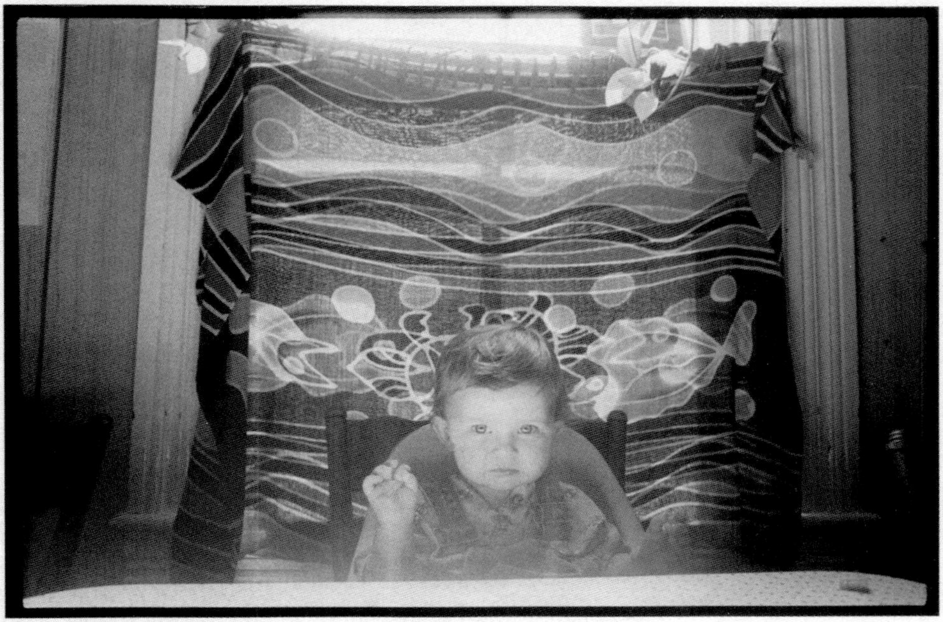

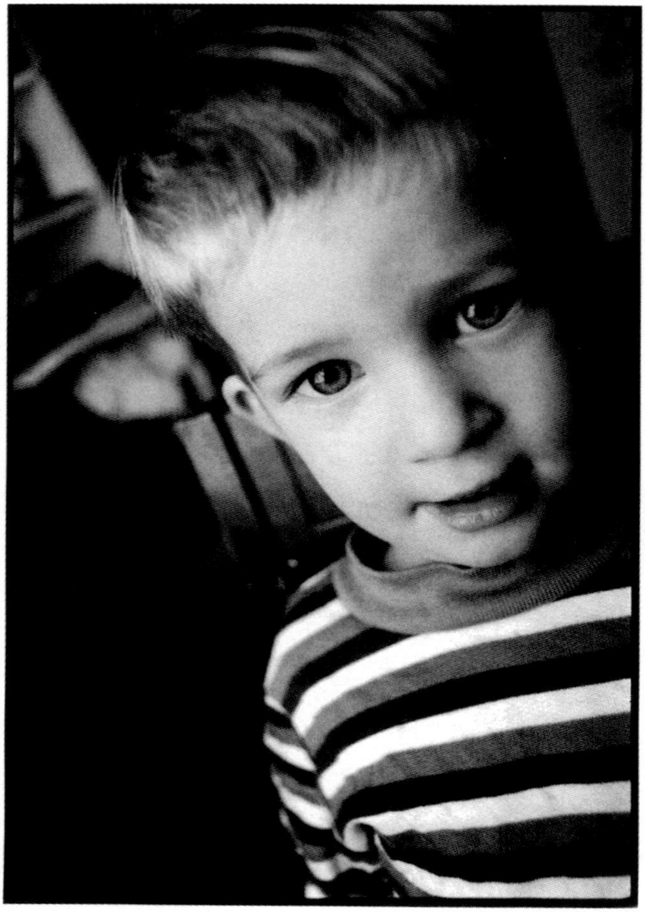

I took a moment to consider… time's up. I was waiting for a sign but none came. Nothing. I can continue or I can go home with my tail between my legs and… where's home, anyway? The best place to begin, or so I've been told, is at the beginning. That is where I'll find you: with a picture, a flashlight and a song.

You, leaving. Or was it me that time? The trouble with the past — with this past — is that it leaks from a barrel and forms a puddle at our feet. A puddle which is in turn soaked up, absorbed, evaporated. The air and the ground below is then filled with faded memories of you, of everyone that lives, of everyone that has ever lived.

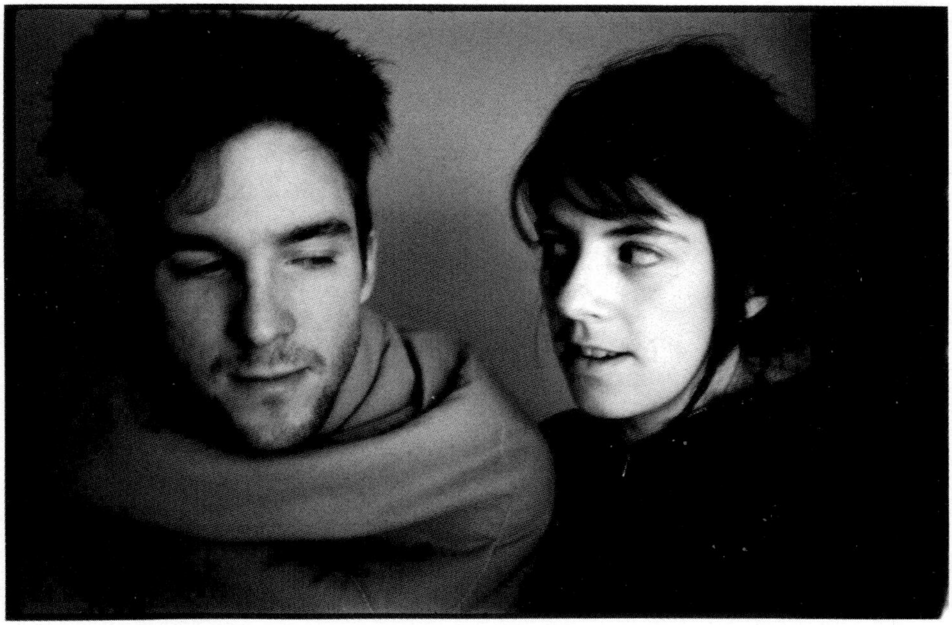

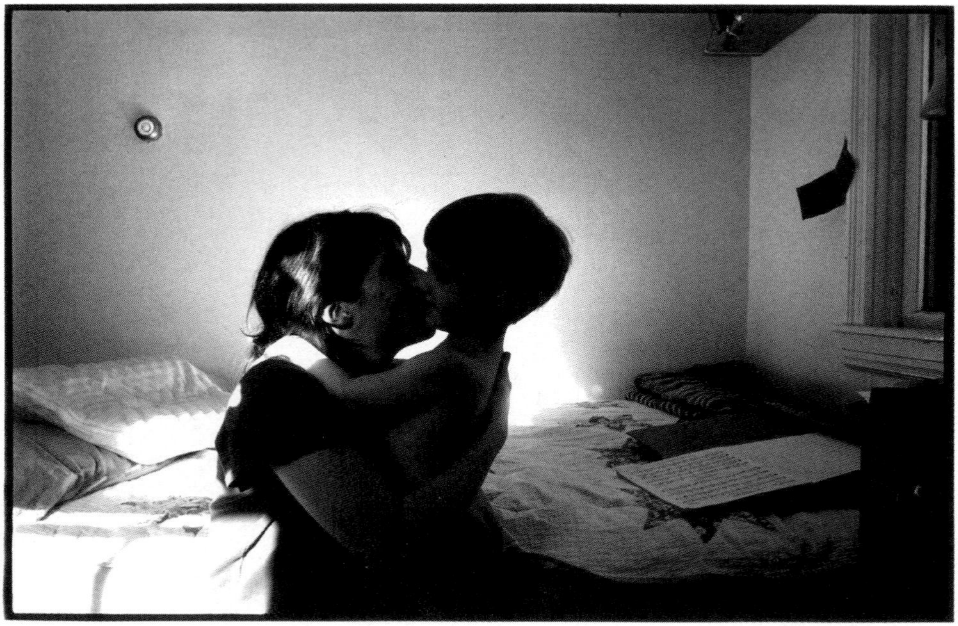

And then there are the times when I feel fine. Watching the boy sleep. Those first few months, I tiptoed into his bedroom and, with my ear close to his mouth, listened for his breath. I always felt a foolish relief when the small, moist warmth of his breath reached my ear — a whispering of his dreams, so quietly. But relief no less.

Two people in bed, their thoughts racing in opposite directions. How would you show that in a photograph?

And what sweet relief it is... There are many times, you whisper, so many. And then you put your finger to my mouth and... Shhhh. Listen. The house is quiet: everything is silenced by the coldness in the room, the snow outside. Slowly, I can make out their breathing and ours and the hum of the refrigerator in the next room. And the sound of the house — it is an old house — creaking and the sound a body makes when it just sits, trying to be quiet. And soon the sounds fill my head and... Do you hear that? Shhhh. Listen.

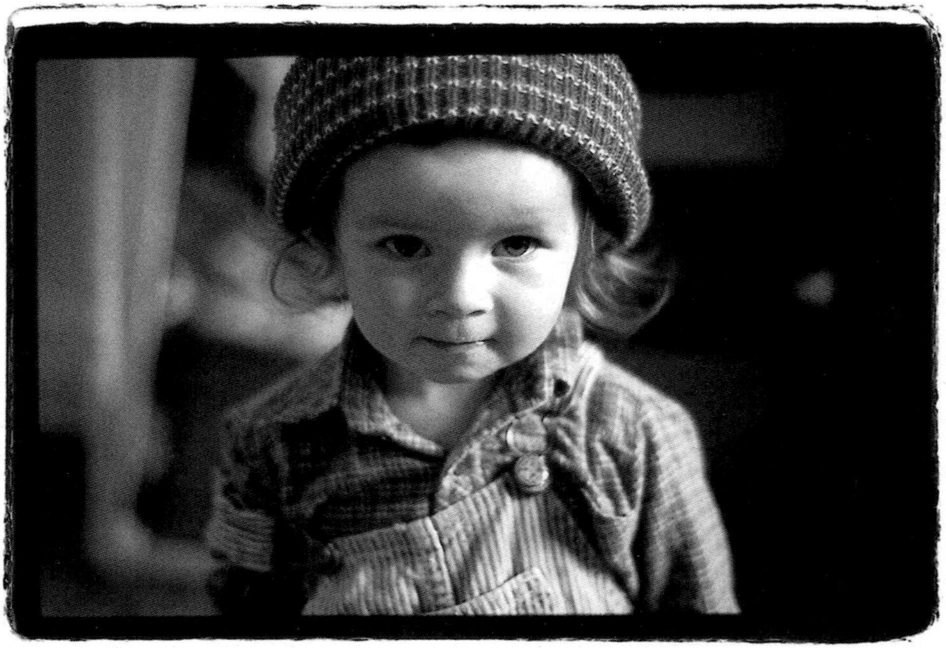

First it was “ma” and then “no,” and then no word was a challenge. We’d laugh at your jokes. You loved that: making us laugh and we loved laughing. Do you remember that? No, no, you wouldn’t, would you? It was a long time ago, wasn’t it? And we’ve changed so much since then. So much has changed since then. But we remember some of it or the best parts, anyway. That is how it works, thank God. And that’s how come we can keep going forward. Like the little train that…

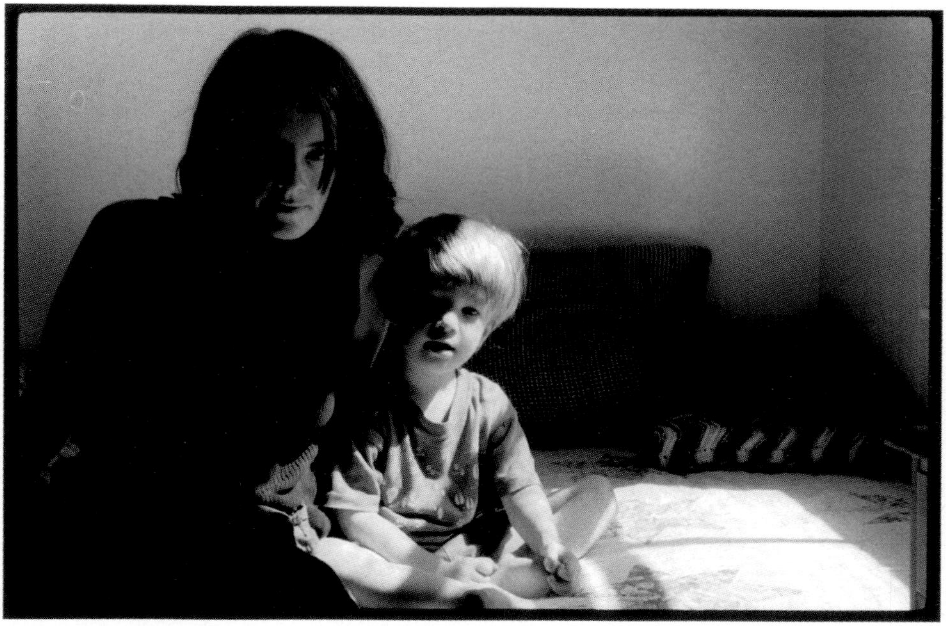

I watched from the window. You didn't look up, even when I knocked on the glass and blew you a kiss. I watched for a long time. I'm not leaving here until you come back, I whispered through the glass. I wouldn't move until then. The dirty patch of driveway where the car had been parked was beginning to whiten. The sky would soon be dark and the snow would stop falling. But it would be a long time. I would have to go to sleep and wake up and go to sleep and wake up and go to sleep and... It would be a long time before you came back.

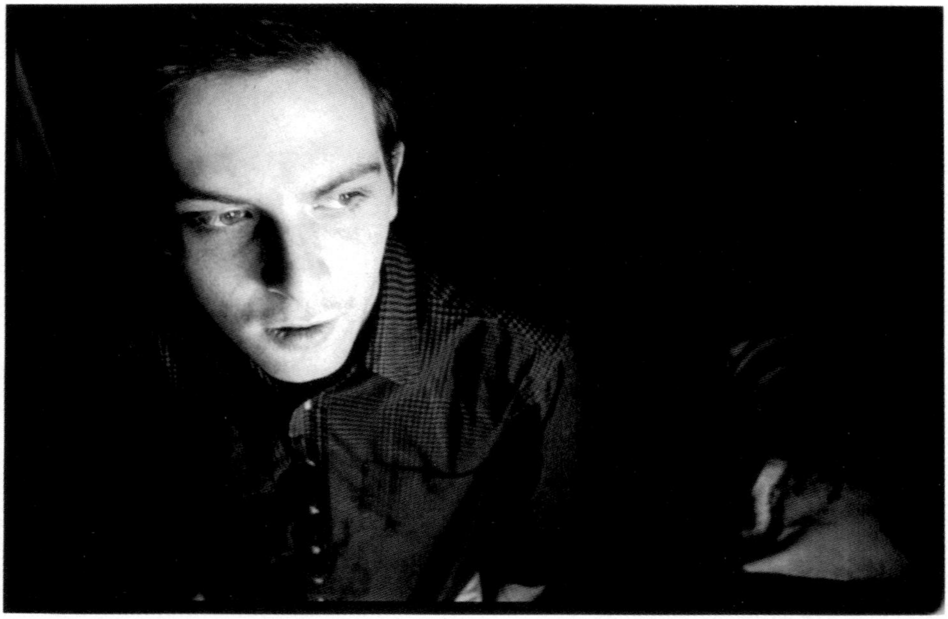

1st man: By now, it has become easy, or at least habitual. I can't imagine any other life. But there was no way I could've known. Not when it started. You just can't predict that kind of thing.

2nd man: Would you have changed anything?

1st man: If I had known?

2nd man: Yes, if you had known.

1st man: No, I guess not. No, I wouldn't have.

Late that night, you drove to the coast. The moon was a hole in the sky above the hills; it was the only light. When you turned down the last stretch of highway and saw the sea — and nothing but darkness in the rear-view mirror — you froze. It was the first time you were confronted by so much nothingness: dark water, dark land. But you continued right down to the water; you put your foot in the ice cold ocean. Straight out ahead, on the water, was a patch of light from the moon — not quite full. And at your feet, the phosphorescence, crackling light every step. There was something else that night, staring off into the dark, that feeling that only comes when your only option is to turn around and retrace your steps, however uncertain.

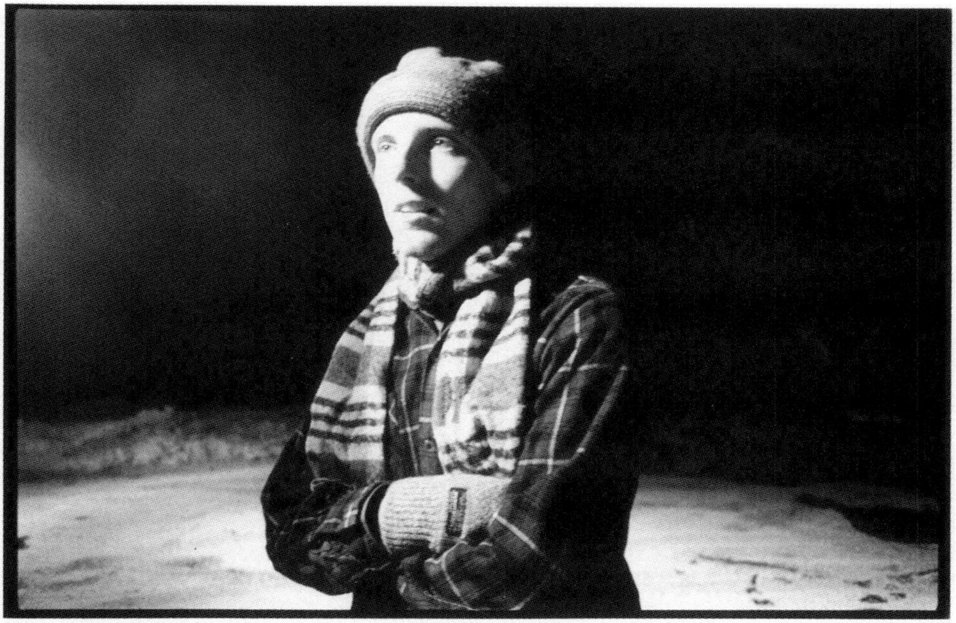

You walked backwards through the sand, keeping your eyes on the darkness ahead; carefully filling every foot print with toe then heel. A child's game: a trail of footprints leading into the water, toward the horizon — you'd fool them all. We had hoped to outrun the blunders and sins of our parents; and this was the only way. We'd lead them down to the water, to the edge of the world. The ice cold shock of it, too much for sins and blunders. The shadows of the past like black clouds sinking into the horizon. But always there to remind us where we came from, and where we're going. Backwards through the sand —

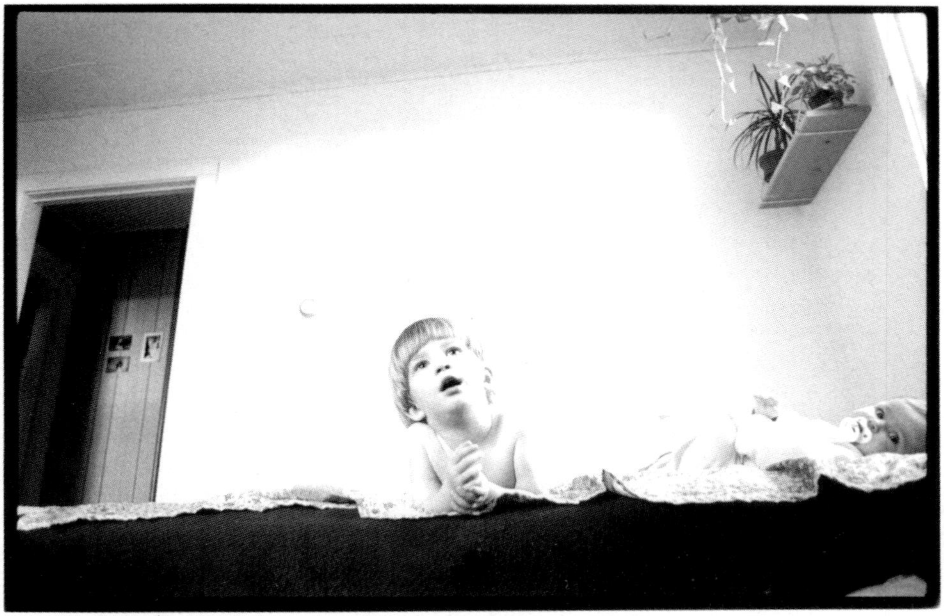

Yes, but *how can I make this year different from the last?*

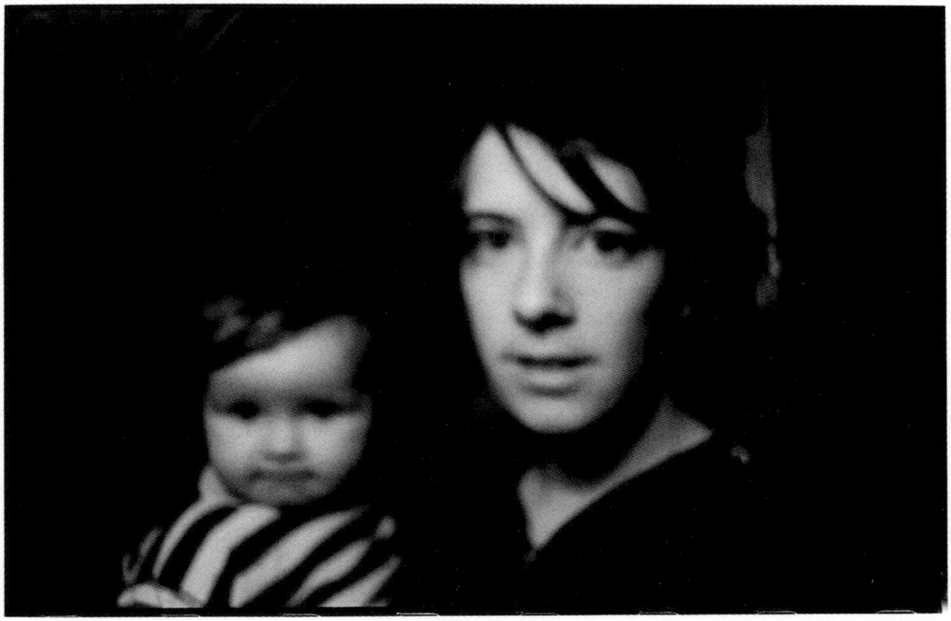

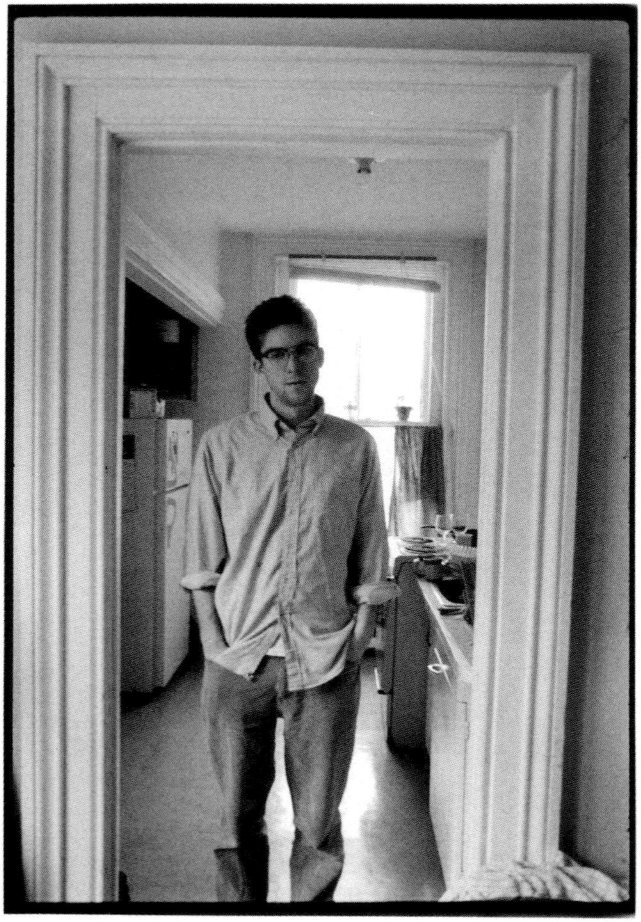

The door will be locked when I get home but I will hear voices on the other side of it. The handle will be cold in my hand; the hallway will smell of smoke and perfume. But I'll linger there, holding on to the handle and thinking about what I'll say — listening and waiting. Before long the door will open and you will smile. You'll look at me and ask, What was the movie about? *A man holding a photograph of a beautiful, young woman was being chased around a table by an old woman carrying a butcher's knife. It was meant to be funny* but…

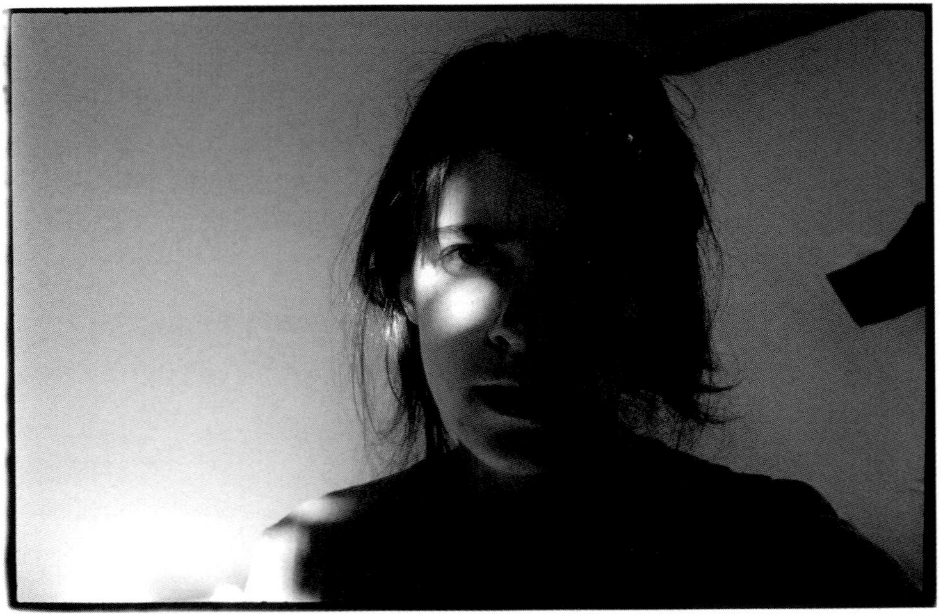

I wasn't sure exactly how long the film had been over. The lights were on and I was staring up at the white screen. I could hear the film slapping against the projector somewhere behind me, round and round and... My eyes adjusted to the brightness of the room. It was then I realised that I was all alone.

(*Things have to change. They do, don't they? And change is good, right? You go on ahead. I'll stay here until I convince myself of this. Go on, I'll catch up later. Hey, I love... No, nothing. Never mind.*)

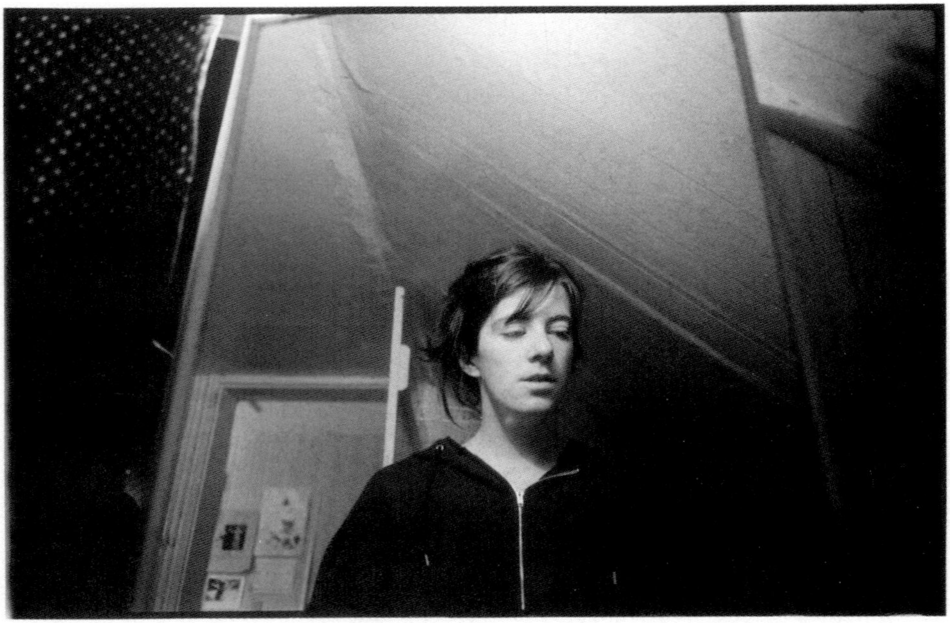

Epilogue

And then it was spring. These memories continue to haunt me. You, wearing a dress, which you so seldom wore, and climbing a tree. A beige dress, a crab apple tree. I stand on the twisted roots below and help you up. The sun is shining in my eyes and I have to squint. You are smiling. Everything is as it should be. No. Maybe it isn't a memory after all but another photograph I've mistaken for a memory. Like so many before. And if you look closely, it becomes plain that you are not smiling at all but looking somewhere over my head toward the horizon… The horizon that — no matter how hard we try — we will never reach, never outrun.

List of Photos

Afterword

You have opened the door and stepped inside. The light which surrounds you is the only light in this gallery. You are holding walls in you hands. *The Longest Winter* is a two-person exhibition, an installation in book form — it is the creation, a collaborative artwork by two artists as true as if two writers wrote a text together. Julie's ink is photosensitive silver halide crystals and/or Ian's camera is his pen — both directed/controlled by eye-hand coordination — as are books.

Artist books, collaborative and solo artist art/photo/text books have been around as long as art and printing. Poetry and photography/art have a strong history together. Whether it's photographs taken to illustrate poems, or poems written about or creatively imagined from within artworks and their artists: From Japanese illustrated haiku scrolls to *Songs of Innocence* by poet-printmaker William Blake. From a French Surrealist duo of a photographer's unsettling photos of hallux paired with Georges Bataille's text to Toronto poet Phlip Arima's *Beneath the Beauty* (Insomniac) with Bonnie Portalance photographs — for many of which Phlip modelled.

Dykelands paired the creative work of Sackville, NB artists and Mount Allison University colleagues — photographer Thaddeus Holownia and poet Douglas Lockhead — in a celebration of their neighbouring Tantramar Marsh.

Lesley Choyce's photo novel, *Magnificant Obsessions*, (Quarry) ties together otherwise unrelated photographs he found in various sources, including, he says, in the trash.

One beautifully-done book is *Written in the Skin: A Poetic Response to AIDS* (Insomniac), an anthology of 37 Canadian poets edited by rob mclennan presented with 41 photographs by Jules de Niverville. Many of the images seem to be casual intimate moments, or they have the haunted feeling of thoughts trailing off... drifting.

Lani Maestro • Shimabuka (Dazibao) is a collaboration by Montréal artist Lani Maestro written around photographs of an installation/performance piece "I'm travelling with a 165-metre mermaid" by Japanese artist Shimabuka. At one point, Lani Maestro writes, "And memory? I make it out of the darkness of the ocean that feels so much like separation."

Memory and the act of creation underlie the whole of *The Longest Winter*. In both the photographs and the text, spheres of self, family and friends, move through distance, isolation and space. Sometimes there is a ray or pool of light. Sometimes only shadow. An unsettling feeling of déjà vu or ennui.

All collaborations begin somewhere. Julie and Ian met several years ago through a common friend — Michael Feuerstack of the Ottawa band Wooden Stars. Julie's label, has released a CD by the band and several 7" vinyl releases by Snailhouse (Michael's solo music project). Their new music collaboration is the *Julie Doiron and The Wooden Stars* CD. Julie, Michael and Ian and their immediate families have grown to be good friends.

When the idea of *The Longest Winter* was gelling, Julie suggested a collaboration with Ian Roy. Ian knew many of the photographs already. His response to Julie's photographs, his words, his fictional narrative, is so clearly described in his Artist Statement (page 7). It seems unnecessary for me to say more than to acknowledge how well the photos and words work together in their playing off of one another.

Julie Doiron's photographs create a composite self portrait. That they are also landscape portraits in their recognition and representation of distance and space adds to their artistry.

Julie Doiron works with a hand-held or surface-mounted, often self-timered, SLR 35mm manual camera and existing light. For self portraits (including ones with her children) the camera, often with a wide-angle lens, is usually held at arm's length. Focus, when the photographer is not behind the camera, is at best a guess, and in some of these portraits the results discredit that near-automatic expectation.

Julie is more spontaneous in how she works than Sally Mann (who works with an 8" x 10" land camera) though both photographers' subjects are their immediate family. There are obvious differences when looking at a body of work: Julie takes more indoor photographs — I believe this is because of climate and Julie's living in urban Canada whereas Mann's work is based around her rural Virginia home; Mann doesn't photograph herself. Julie says she takes self portraits because of a lack of other subjects, "I'm the only one who doesn't mind being photographed frequently."

Her full-frame, uncropped silver print images have the magic of Robert Frank or Garry Winogrand's work. Her self portraits are more immediate, more honest than Maplethorpe's or, as Johnston says in *Photography Speaks* (Arperture/The Chrysler Museum), Cindy Sherman's "thematically focused groups of imagined staged environmental portraits in which the artist herself acts as subject."

In her photographs, Julie, her family and friends, are very real and engagingly immediate. These photographs capture a wide spectrum of emotion, feeling and state of mind: loneliness, love, confusion, fun, chill, wonder, challenge, worry, confrontation, resignation, comfort and much more...

— Joe Blades
Publisher and photographer

About the Authors

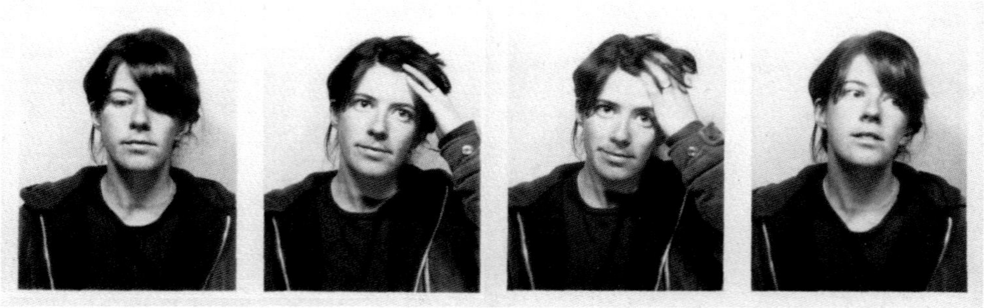

Julie Doiron, originally from Moncton, New Brunswick, is best-known for her years as bassist, vocalist and songwriter with Canadian indie music darlings Eric's Trip. Her newest CD, *Julie Doiron and the Wooden Stars*, to be released in September 1999, is on her own Sappy Records label. Julie and her husband, artist Jon Claytor, have two children, Charlotte and Ben, and they live in Montréal.

Julie Doiron studied photography with Thaddeus Holownia at Mount Allison University in Sackville, New Brunswick. In addition to their inclusion in varous publications, she has had solo exhibitions of her photo prints.

For up-to-date info on her music shows, store appearances, CD releases and much more, join Julie Doiron's e-mail list at: www.onelist.com/subscribe/Julie_doiron or write to: Sappy Records, Box 4 Stn A, Fredericton NB E3B 4Y2, Canada.

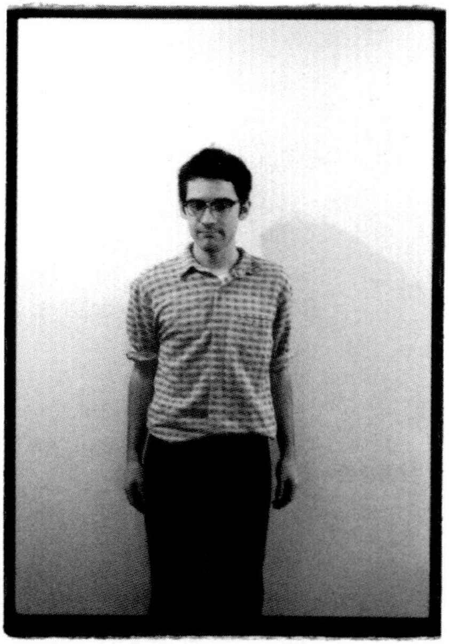

Ian Roy is an Ottawa Valley writer who has a BA in English from the University of Ottawa. Ian and his wife, Sarah, have one child, Max. Ian has published in poetry and fiction in literary periodicals including *Arc*, *New Muse of Contempt* and *Geist* as well as several already hard-to-find Sappy chapbooks. Currently working on a collaborative filmscript, *The Longest Winter* is Ian's first book.

A Selection of Our Titles in Print

A Lad from Brantford (David Adams Richards) essays	0-921411-25-1	11.95
All the Other Phil Thompsons Are Dead (Phil Thompson) poetry	1-896647-05-7	12.95
A View from the Bucket: A Grand Lake and McNabs Island Memoir (Jean Redekopp) memoir, history	0-921411-52-9	14.95
Best in Life: A Guide to Managing Your Relationships ... (Ted Mouradian) self-improvement, business	0-921411-55-3	17.95
Cover Makes a Set (Joe Blades) poetry	0-919957-60-9	8.95
Crossroads Cant (Mary Elizabeth Grace, Mark Seabrook, Shafiq, Ann Shin. Joe Blades, editor) poetry	0-921411-48-0	13.95
Dark Seasons (Georg Trakl; Robin Skelton, trans.) poetry	0-921411-22-7	10.95
for a cappuccino on Bloor (kath macLean) poetry	0-921411-74-X	13.95
Gift of Screws (Robin Hannah) poetry	0-921411-56-1	12.95
Fredericton Past: A Photo Album (Joe Blades, editor)	0-921411-73-1	16.95
Heaven of Small Moments (Allan Cooper) poetry	0-921411-79-0	12.95
Herbarium of Souls (Vladimir Tasic) short fiction	0-921411-72-3	14.95
I Hope It Don't Rain Tonight (Phillip Igloliorti) poetry	0-921411-57-X	11.95
Like Minds (Shannon Friesen) short fiction	0-921411-81-2	14.95
Manitoba highway map (rob mclennan) poetry	0-921411-89-8	13.95
Memories of Sandy Point, St. George's Bay, Newfoundland (Phyllis Pieroway) memoir, history	0-921411-33-2	14.95
New Power (Christine Lowther) poetry	0-921411-94-4	11.95
Notes on drowning (rob mclennan) poetry	0-921411-75-8	13.95
Open 24 Hours (Anne Burke, D.C. Reid, Brenda Niskala Joe Blades, rob mclennan) poetry	0-921411-64-2	13.95
Poems for Little Cataraqui (Eric Folsom) poetry	0-921411-28-6	10.95
Railway Station (karl wendt) poetry	0-921411-82-0	11.95
Rum River (Raymond Fraser) short fiction	0-921411-61-8	16.95
Seeing the World with One Eye (Edward Gates) poetry	0-921411-69-3	12.95
Song of the Vulgar Starling (Eric Miller) poetry	0-921411-93-6	14.95
Speaking Through Jagged Rock (Connie Fife) poetry	0-921411-99-5	12.95
Tales for an Urban Sky (Alice Major) poetry	1-896647-11-1	13.95
The Best Lack All (Tom Schmidt) poetry	0-921411-37-5	12.95
The Longest Winter (Julie Doiron, Ian Roy) photos & fiction	0-921411-95-2	18.69
Túnel de proa verde / Tunnel of the Green Prow (Nela Rio; Hugh Hazelton, translator) poetry	0-921411-80-4	13.95
Wharves and Breakwaters of Yarmouth County, Nova Scotia (Sarah Petite) art/nonfiction	1-896647-13-8	17.95
What Morning Illuminates (Suzanne Hancock) poetry	1-896647-18-9	4.95
What Was Always Hers (Uma Parameswaran) fiction	1-896647-12-X	17.95

www.brokenjaw.com hosts our current catalogue. Direct from us, all individual orders must be prepaid. Canadian orders must add 7% GST/HST (Revenue Canada Business Number 12489 7943 RT0001). BROKEN JAW PRESS, Box 596 Stn A, Fredericton NB E3B 5A6, Canada. Tel/fax 506 454-5127.
Canadian trade sales representation: LITERARY PRESS GROUP OF CANADA, 401-110 Eglinton Av W, Toronto ON M4R 1A3. Tel 416 483-1321, fax 416 483-2510. www.lpg.ca info@lpg.ca
Credit card orders, trade order fulfilment: GENERAL DISTRIBUTION SERVICES, 325 Humber College Blvd, Toronto ON M9W 7C3. Atlantic, Western Canada and NW Ontario tel 1-800-387-0172; Toronto tel 416 213-1919; fax 416 213-1917; customer.service@ccmailgw.genpub.co
GENERAL DISTRIBUTION SERVICES, Box 386, Lewiston NY 14092 - 0386. tel 1-800-805-1083, fax 1-800-481-6207, gdsinc@genpub.com , Pubnet 6307949.